YOU HOLD IN YOUR HANDS THE M[...]
HOLIDAY TRADITION NO ONE ASKED FOR:
24 DAYS OF MEANINGLESS INFORMATION.

EACH DAY, OPEN A PAGE
AND FILL YOUR BRAIN WITH FACTS SO UNNECESSARY,
YOU'LL FORGET THEM BEFORE YOU FLUSH.

Merry sitting.

CW01455189

Matt Wild. All rights Reserved.
No part of this publication may be reproduced, distributed or transmitted in any form or be
any means, including photocopying, recording or other electronic or mechanical method,
without prior written permission of the publisher, except in the case of brief quotation
embodied in critical reviews and certain other noncommercial uses permitted by copyright law.

DAY 1

The Beginning of Christmas Chaos

Main Trivia #1: *Santa wasn't always red*

Before Coca-Cola dressed him in his now-iconic red suit, Santa Claus was a true fashion chameleon.

In 19th-century illustrations, he appeared in green, blue, brown, or tan — sometimes a thin, bishop-like figure, other times a woodland spirit wrapped in fur.

Then, in 1931, Coca-Cola hired artist Haddon Sundblom to create a jollier, rounder Santa for their winter ads. His rosy cheeks and warm smile became so beloved that other brands copied the look — and soon, the red-suited Santa was here to stay.

💪 **Christmas Table Flex:**

"Santa's red outfit is basically a marketing success story from the 1930s, before that, he was just a guy in random colors wandering through chimneys."

Bonus Fact Corner: Quick Hits for the Curious

- The average Christmas tree has over 300,000 needles.
- "Jingle Bells" was the first song ever played in space (by astronauts aboard Gemini 6, 1965).
- The biggest snowflake ever recorded was 15 inches wide, found in Montana in 1887 — allegedly.
- In Germany, kids who behave get chocolate in their shoes from St. Nicholas. Those who don't might get a stick from Krampus.

Mini Thought:

If you ever feel stuck in your career, just remember: even santa needed a rebrand.

Leaving snacks for Santa might seem like a simple tradition, but it began during hard times.

In the Great Depression of the 1930s, American parents taught generosity by having children share what little they had — leaving cookies and milk as a thank-you gesture.

In the U.K. and Ireland, Santa gets mince pies and sherry (a risky combo for a sleigh ride), while Danish kids offer rice pudding to nisse, a helpful Christmas gnome.

So next time you reach for a sugar cookie, remember — it all started as a moral lesson and turned into Santa's favorite cheat day.

Christmas Table Flex:

"Fun fact - cookies for Santa were invented during the Great Depression to teach kids gratitude. The sherry was just a bonus."

TOTALLY USELESS RECORDS YOU DIDN'T ASK FOR:

46 toilet seats broken by the head in one minute – One man smashed 46 wooden toilet seats using nothing but his forehead. It's impressive, confusing, and definitely not covered by health insurance.

Most snails on the face for 10 seconds: 43 snails - A boy placed 43 live snails all over his face and kept them there for 10 full seconds. No glue, no tricks, just pure slimy determination. Why? We still don't know.

Loudest burp (female): 107.3 dB – This burp was so loud it could compete with a motorbike. Family dinners will never be the same.

🧪 BATHROOM SCIENCE: *The truth about glitter*

That festive sparkle on cards, wrapping paper, and ornaments? It's made of microplastic coated with aluminum. A single pinch can release over 100,000 tiny particles and pollute up to 30 gallons (115 liters) of water.

Some countries, like the U.K. and New Zealand, have banned certain glitters — but let's face it, sparkle season isn't going anywhere. So if your bathroom ends up shimmering after gift-wrapping, just smile and call it a touch of "holiday magic."

💭?? Toilet Thought of the Day:

"If Santa really came down every chimney, he'd leave with glitter in his beard for the rest of eternity."

TRUE OR FALSE

? The first artificial Christmas trees were made of goose feathers

The world's tallest Christmas tree was in Finland. ?

? "Jingle Bells" was originally written for Thanksgiving.

Candy canes were invented by a choirmaster to keep kids quiet during mass.

End-of-Day Wisdom

You've officially made it through Day 1. You've learned that Santa's style was corporate, his diet questionable, and glitter is secretly evil. Tomorrow, the trivia tour goes global - but for now, take pride in knowing you're already the smartest person in the bathroom.

DAY 2

Festive Facts from Around the World

Main Trivia #1: *In Japan, Christmas tastes like fried chicken.*

In Japan, Christmas Eve means one thing – KFC.

Since 1974, when the chain launched its "Kentucky for Christmas" campaign, fried chicken has become the country's go-to festive meal.

With no traditional Christmas dishes at the time, Japan embraced the idea of a "Western-style" feast – crispy chicken, coleslaw, and a red bucket.

The campaign was such a hit that people still pre-order weeks ahead, and some KFCs even sell out by Christmas Eve.

Proof that great marketing can turn fast food into a holiday tradition.

Christmas Table Flex:

"Japan's Christmas tradition? Buckets of KFC. Proof that genius marketing beats grandma's cooking."

Bonus Fact Corner: Cultural Surprises

- In some parts of South Africa, families eat fried Christmas caterpillars – a delicacy said to bring luck and prosperity for the new year.
- In Greenland, people traditionally enjoy a dish called kiviak: raw seabird meat fermented inside a seal's skin. Definitely not KFC.
- Australians celebrate Christmas in the middle of summer, often barbecuing on the beach while wearing Santa hats and sunscreen.

In Norway, Christmas Eve isn't just about gifts – it's about hiding brooms.

Old folklore says that on Christmas Eve, witches and mischievous spirits fly through the sky looking for broomsticks to steal. To stop them, families tuck away every broom, mop, and even the vacuum.

Today it's a playful tradition – kids make sure the brooms are "safe," while parents sometimes hide one just for fun.

So if you wake up in Norway and can't find your broom, relax – it's not a chore day, it's Christmas magic.

Christmas Table Flex:

"In Norway, people hide their brooms so witches don't borrow them on Christmas Eve. It's basically anti-theft for magical transportation."

TOTALLY USELESS RECORDS YOU DIDN'T ASK FOR:

Greatest extent of reverse pedestrianism: about 12,875 km walked backwards – One man walked backwards across multiple countries. It took months, lots of balance, and probably very strong calves.

Across many parts of Europe – including cities such as Rome, Italy – you'll often find public toilets that require a coin (usually €0.50 to €1) to enter. The "Pay-to-Pee" model is surprisingly common.

Publication containing the most useless inventions: two books of "Unuseless Japanese Inventions" – A creator compiled books full of inventions no one needs, like chopsticks with a fan. Completely pointless, yet proudly record-breaking.

FUN FACT QUICKFIRE:
Around the World in One Toilet Sit

- In Italy, kids get sweets from La Befana – a kind old witch who visits on January 6th.
- In Iceland, 13 mischievous Yule Lads leave gifts or rotten potatoes, depending on behavior.
- In Mexico, radishes become art during Noche de Rábanos (Night of the Radishes).
- In the Philippines, the Giant Lantern Festival lights up San Fernando with lanterns as big as cars.
- In Germany, kids leave shoes out on December 5th for St. Nicholas – who fills them with candy... or a stick.
- In Ukraine, spiders are a symbol of Christmas luck – legend says their webs once turned into gold and silver on a poor widow's tree.
- In Sweden, the city of Gävle builds a 40-foot straw Yule Goat each year – and pranksters keep trying to burn it down.

MINI QUIZ - MATCH THE TRADITION TO THE COUNTRY

A. KFC for Christmas dinner
B. Burning a giant straw goat
C. Lucky spider webs on the tree
D. Hiding brooms from witches
E. The Night of the Radishes

1. Japan
2. Sweden
3. Ukraine
4. Norway
5. Mexico

End-of-Day Wisdom

Christmas looks different around the world - from glittering spiders to fried chicken and flaming straw goats - but it all celebrates the same things: joy, togetherness, and a bit of chaos. So raise a toast to cultural creativity - you've survived Day 2 of the toilet advent calendar and now know more about Christmas than 99% of your dinner table.

DAY 3
Festive Feasts, Drinks, and Disasters

Main Trivia #1: *The Christmas dinner that fed 3,000 people*

In 2019, a British pub in South Yorkshire served Christmas dinner to over 3,000 people in one day.

It took 200 staff, 2,500 roast potatoes, 1,800 Yorkshire puddings, and enough gravy to fill a pool. The chef started at 4 a.m. and didn't sit down until closing.

The tradition began when the owner vowed no one should eat alone on Christmas — and it grew into a huge community feast. Even the leftovers were boxed up and delivered to hospitals and shelters.

Christmas Table Flex:

"A single British pub fed 3,000 people on Christmas. Turns out Santa's workshop also serves pints."

Fruitcake was used as wedding cake in Victorian England because it lasted so long. Some couples even kept a slice until their first anniversary - and still ate it.

In 2018, Venezuela set a Guinness World Record by serving over 15,000 people a Christmas meal in a single event.

The first printed recipe for Christmas pudding appeared in Eliza Acton's 1845 cookbook, one year before A Christmas Carol made the dessert world-famous.

In 2020, scientists in Germany created a lab-grown Christmas turkey using cultured cells. It reportedly tasted "strangely smooth".

Eggnog has always been a bit of a troublemaker.
This rich blend of milk, cream, eggs, sugar, and booze started in 17th-century England as a winter punch, then sailed to America, where colonists added rum.
But in 1826, it caused chaos – West Point cadets smuggled whiskey for a Christmas party, sparking the infamous Eggnog Riot that ended with smashed windows and 20 arrests.
Today, it's a festive classic with a health warning – if it's not pasteurized, the only riot might be in your stomach.

🦾 **Christmas Table Flex:**

"Eggnog once caused an actual riot at West Point. That's some serious holiday spirit."

TOTALLY USELESS RECORDS YOU DIDN'T ASK FOR:

Most number-typing: from "one" to "one million" in words (not digits), took 16 years – Someone spent 16 years typing every number from one to one million using only words. It's the world's slowest countdown.

In Indonesia, the left hand is conventionally used for toilet hygiene; using the right hand for personal cleansing is considered inappropriate.

Most watermelons chopped on someone's stomach in one minute – a very brave volunteer lies still while another person slices watermelons on their belly with a machete.
The Guinness World Record is 78 melons in 60 seconds – half circus act, half panic attack.

Bonus Fact Corner: Holiday Food Oddities

In England, mince pies once contained real meat – lamb, beef, or venison mixed with fruit and spices. Over time, sugar took over, and by the 19th century they turned into the sweet version we eat today.

Christmas pudding also started as a meaty stew before evolving into a dense, boozy dessert. British sailors even took it overseas, since the suet kept it fresh for months.

In Greenland, locals serve mattak – raw whale skin with a layer of blubber, said to taste like coconut.

Iceland enjoys laufabrauð – thin, crispy bread with intricate cut-out designs, fried golden and served with butter.

Italy celebrates with panettone, a tall, fluffy cake filled with raisins and candied fruit – now even found in ice cream and cocktails.

France finishes with Bûche de Noël, a chocolate log cake decorated with meringue mushrooms or tiny sugar saws.

In Poland, Wigilia dinner includes twelve meatless dishes, one for each apostle, starting with sharing opłatek (a Christmas wafer) and warm wishes.

End-of-Day Wisdom

Christmas food traditions prove one thing: humans will eat almost anything if it's covered in butter, sugar, or nostalgia. From fried chicken in Japan to flaming puddings in Britain, our holiday tables mix history, chaos, and joy.

You've survived Day 3 of the Toilet Advent Calendar - and earned the right to judge everyone's cooking this Christmas.

DAY 4

Christmas Legends & Strange Beliefs

Main Trivia #1: The Icelandic Yule Cat

In Iceland, there's a mythical giant cat called Jólakötturinn, or the Yule Cat, who prowls the snowy countryside at Christmas. He doesn't care about your behavior; he cares about your clothes, and legend says he eats anyone who doesn't get something new to wear before Christmas Eve.

The tale began as motivation to work hard during winter, when those who helped with wool production earned new garments while the lazy risked becoming cat food.

Today, the Yule Cat is part of Icelandic holiday lore, glowing in lights over Reykjavik – massive, festive, and hopefully full.

Christmas Table Flex:

"In Iceland, there's a giant cat that eats people who don't get new clothes for Christmas. Fashion really is deadly."

TOTALLY USELESS RECORDS YOU DIDN'T ASK FOR:

Fastest time to cross a greased pole: 3.04 seconds – A competitor slid across a long pole coated in grease. It's slippery chaos, but surprisingly athletic.

In China and South Korea, many public toilets do not supply toilet paper, so travellers are advised to bring their own tissues.

Mini Thought:

Suddenly, new pajamas on Christmas Eve don't seem like a bad deal.

Before Christmas became all snow and cheer, it had a spooky side.

In Victorian England, families spent Christmas Eve telling ghost stories by the fire, long before Halloween took over the scares.

Charles Dickens' A Christmas Carol came from this very tradition, and 19th-century magazines even printed "Christmas ghost specials" full of eerie tales.

So next time you watch The Muppet Christmas Carol, remember — it's not just festive, it's frightfully traditional.

💪 Christmas Table Flex:

"The Victorians loved telling ghost stories on Christmas Eve. 'A Christmas Carol' was basically the Netflix horror of its time."

Bonus Fact Corner:
Beliefs You Didn't Know Were Festive

- In some Slavic countries, it's considered bad luck to clean on Christmas Day – you might sweep away the season's blessings.
- In Ireland, people leave out a slice of Christmas cake and a candle in the window for Mary and Joseph – a gesture of welcome for travelers.
- In Wales, the eerie Mari Lwyd (a horse skull decorated with ribbons) goes door to door singing songs and challenging people to rhyme battles. The winner gets to enter the house for food and drink.

FUN FACT QUICKFIRE:
Myths & Magic from Around the World

- In Austria and Germany, Krampus – Santa's horned sidekick – chases naughty kids on December 5th with chains and sticks. Locals still celebrate Krampusnacht with parades full of scary costumes and ringing bells.
- In Italy, La Befana, a kind old witch, flies on her broom on January 6th, leaving sweets for good children and coal for the naughty. Legend says she missed baby Jesus because she was too busy cleaning.
- In Greece, goblin-like Kallikantzaroi sneak into homes during the Twelve Days of Christmas to cause chaos, disappearing after the priest blesses the house.
- In Ukraine, families decorate their trees with spider webs for good luck – inspired by the legend of the Christmas Spider.
- In Catalonia, there's a "pooping log" called Tió de Nadal. Families feed it snacks, then hit it with sticks until it "poops" out presents.
- In Germany, kids hang stockings for St. Nicholas on December 6th – and hope his grumpy helper, Knecht Ruprecht, doesn't show up with a stick.
- In the Philippines, people light colorful parol lanterns and gather for Noche Buena, a feast believed to bring blessings for the year ahead.

End-of-Day Wisdom

Every country has its own kind of Christmas magic - from kind witches to scary gift inspectors and fashion-loving cats. These myths may sound strange, but they all reflect the same thing: our need to bring mystery and meaning to the darkest nights of the year. You've made it through Day 4 of your toilet advent calendar. Sleep tight, hide your broom, and maybe treat yourself to new socks - just to be safe.

DAY 5

The Magic of Gifts, Trees & Decorations

Main Trivia #1: How Gifting Began

The tradition of giving Christmas gifts began as a tribute to the Three Wise Men, who brought gold, frankincense, and myrrh to baby Jesus. For centuries, however, gift-giving wasn't a personal tradition – it was either symbolic, meant for royalty and clergy, or charitable, given by the wealthy to the poor.

Personal gift exchanges only took off in the 1800s, when Christmas started shifting into a family-focused holiday. Industrialization made toys and books more affordable, and shops jumped on the sleigh with festive deals and "Christmas specials." By the early 1900s, Santa had officially traded the church for the shop window.

💪 Christmas Table Flex:

"The first Christmas gifts weren't from Santa - they were luxury baby shower presents from the Three Wise Men."

TOTALLY USELESS RECORDS YOU DIDN'T ASK FOR:

Most spoons balanced on the face: 31 spoons – One person managed to stick 31 spoons onto their face at the same time. No glue, just skill… or maybe good skin stickiness.

Most Guinness world records held at once: over 120 – one individual has held more than 120 different world records at the same time. Basically, they collect world records like Pokemon.

Mini Thought:

From gold and myrrh to socks and candles - progress?

Before wrapping paper existed, people covered gifts in fabric, plain paper, or even newspaper.

Then, in 1917, two brothers running a stationery store in Kansas City accidentally ran out of tissue paper. Desperate to please their customers, they sold fancy French envelope liners instead – glossy, colorful sheets originally meant for letter writing.

People loved it. The next year, they printed their own versions and invented what we now know as commercial wrapping paper.

Those brothers? Joyce and Rollie Hall, founders of Hallmark.

💪 Christmas Table Flex:

"Wrapping paper was invented by accident when a shop ran out of tissue paper. Hallmark turned a crisis into an empire."

FUN FACT QUICKFIRE: *Decorations Around the World*

- In Mexico, families decorate with paper lanterns called farolitos, and some towns display giant illuminated nativity scenes in the streets.
- In Japan, Christmas trees are often decorated with origami cranes for peace and luck.
- In Sweden, people place candles in every window to symbolize welcoming light during the darkest days of winter.
- In Ukraine, people hide a small decorative spider web on the tree for good luck – a nod to the Christmas Spider legend.
- In Australia, trees are often adorned with seashells and lights shaped like tropical flowers, since Christmas falls in the middle of summer.

Bonus Fact Corner: The Odd Side of Gifts & Giving

In ancient Rome, during the festival of Saturnalia, people exchanged candles, dolls, and gag gifts – possibly the earliest Secret Santa.

The most expensive Christmas tree ever decorated was displayed in Spain in 2019. It was covered in diamonds, sapphires, and 24-karat gold and valued at over $15 million.

The world's largest Christmas present was the Statue of Liberty, gifted by France to the United States in 1886. It just took a few extra years to unwrap and assemble.

Every year, the city of Oslo sends a giant Christmas tree to London's Trafalgar Square as thanks for Britain's help during World War II.

In some parts of Germany, children don't open gifts on December 25th but on Christmas Eve – a tradition known as Bescherung.

⁉️ Toilet Thought of the Day:

"Decorations say more about your geography than your personality. In Australia, Santa wears flip-flops; in Sweden, he's a candle salesman."

End-of-Day Wisdom

From wrapping-paper empires to handmade gifts, many Christmas traditions began as happy accidents.

The magic isn't in perfection but in thoughtfulness - every messy tree or glowing candle says, I thought of you.

You've reached the halfway point of your toilet advent calendar.

Tomorrow, it's time to see what happens when Christmas goes delightfully wrong.

DAY 6

Christmas Disasters & Funny Records

Main Trivia #1: *New York's Hottest Christmas Ever*

It was meant to be the most beautiful tree in America – 65 feet tall, covered in 2,500 lights at Rockefeller Center. But early on Christmas Day 1956, faulty wiring sparked a fire, and the massive tree went up in flames. Firefighters arrived fast, but the top half was already gone, leaving a charred trunk behind. No one was hurt, and within 24 hours the city replaced it – the press called it "the miracle of the smoking spruce."

💪 Christmas Table Flex:

"In 1956, the Rockefeller Center tree caught fire. They replaced it the next day. Classic New York."

TOTALLY USELESS RECORDS YOU DIDN'T ASK FOR

A Spanish collector amassed 5,025 dog-figurines, soft toys and walking sticks as a tribute, and this large collection was officially recognised by Guinness World Records as the largest collection of canine-related items.

In some Swiss apartment buildings you mustn't flush the toilet after 10 P.M., because flushing is considered noise pollution at night and may disturb neighbours.

Strangest diet: consumed a Cessna 150 light aircraft – Michel Lotito is recorded for a "strangest diet", including eating a Cessna 150 plane over time.

Bonus Fact Corner: Quick Hits for the Curious

Big Ben, 1962 – On New Year's Eve 1962–63, Big Ben chimed about ten minutes late because heavy snow and ice jammed its clock hands.

Trafalgar Square Tree, 2021 – The 2021 Christmas tree gifted by Norway to London was widely criticised for its sparse, "threadbare" appearance, causing social media jokes and complaints.

Rockefeller Center Owl Rescue, 2020 – In November 2020 an owl was discovered tucked inside the Christmas tree at Rockefeller Center, New York, and was rescued by wildlife officials.

Gävle Goat, Sweden – Each year since 1966 a giant straw goat is erected in Gävle for Christmas, and most years it is partially or fully destroyed by arsonists despite security measures.

MAIN TRIVIA #2: The Turkey Fryer Fire Epidemic

In the U.S., deep-frying turkeys has become a Thanksgiving and Christmas trend – and a yearly disaster.
Every December, fire departments across the country report over 1,000 fryer-related fires caused by frozen turkeys dropped into boiling oil.
The explosions are so common that the National Fire Protection Association releases an annual warning video called "Don't Fry Your House This Holiday."
Some of the fires are spectacular:
In 2006, one Florida family's fryer explosion destroyed their garage and two cars. In 2019, a Texas homeowner accidentally launched his turkey 10 feet into the air and set the roof ablaze.

💪 Christmas Table Flex:

"America's most dangerous Christmas tradition is deep-frying frozen turkeys. The smell of smoke? That's just the holiday spirit leaving your kitchen."

TRUE or FALSE

? The first Christmas card was sent in 1843.

"Silent Night" was written in German, not Latin. ?

Rudolph was invented by Coca-Cola. ?

In Poland, people open gifts on Christmas Eve, not Christmas Day.

MINI QUIZ - GUESS THE RECORD!
Which of these is the real Guinness World Record?

A. Largest Christmas sweater – 30 meters wide
B. Tallest snowman – 122 feet tall
C. Fastest snowball throw – 300 km/h

End-of-Day Wisdom

Every Christmas has at least one small disaster - a burnt turkey, a broken ornament, or wrapping paper chaos.

But those are the stories that make the holidays unforgettable. Perfection is overrated; laughter is the real tradition.

You've completed Day 6 of your Toilet Advent Calendar.

If your own Christmas goes up in flames, just remember - you're in excellent company.

Christmas Movies & Music You Thought You Knew

Main Trivia #1: *"Home Alone" almost never got made*

It's one of the most beloved Christmas movies ever, but Home Alone was nearly cancelled halfway through filming. The studio originally financing it, Warner Bros., pulled out when the budget went over $10 million. Luckily, 20th Century Fox quietly stepped in and took over without stopping production. Filming continued in an abandoned high school in Illinois — the flooded basement scene was shot in the school's swimming pool, converted into a fake house set. The movie went on to earn over $475 million worldwide, becoming the highest-grossing comedy of the 1990s.

💪 Christmas Table Flex:

"Home Alone was shot in an abandoned high school, and the studio switched mid-film. Basically, it's the most successful accident in movie history."

Bonus Fact Corner: Soundtrack Surprises

- Have Yourself a Merry Little Christmas originally had darker lyrics ("It may be your last"), but they were softened for Meet Me in St. Louis to sound more hopeful.
- Do They Know It's Christmas? by Band Aid was recorded in one day in 1984 by more than 40 artists — it raised millions for famine relief in Ethiopia.
- White Christmas by Bing Crosby remains the best-selling single by a solo artist in history.

Mini Thought:
Even movie miracles start with a budget problem.

Today, It's a Wonderful Life is a must-watch Christmas classic, but when it came out in 1946, it was a box-office disappointment.

Critics liked it, but postwar audiences didn't – the story of financial ruin and angels felt too heavy at the time.

It stayed forgotten until a copyright lapse in the 1970s made it free to air on TV.

Local stations started showing it every Christmas, and that's how it became a holiday legend.

BOX OFFICE

💪 Christmas Table Flex:

"It's a Wonderful Life flopped in theaters, then became a classic by accident. Guess angels aren't the only ones getting second chances."

TOTALLY USELESS RECORDS YOU DIDN'T ASK FOR:

In Japan, public toilet etiquette emphasises quiet, cleanliness and consideration: in some places sound-masking devices are used so that users' natural sounds are hidden.

Most chopsticks put into a beard in one minute (team of two): 104 chopsticks - Two people teamed up and inserted 104 chopsticks into a beard in 60 seconds.

The world's tallest dog (Reggie, a Great Dane) and the world's shortest dog (Pearl, a Chihuahua) met for a special playdate arranged by Guinness World Records, showcasing size extremes with a friendly twist.

📯 Toilet Thought of the Day:

"'Have Yourself a Merry Little Christmas' was originally depressing enough to ruin any dinner party."

TRUE OR FALSE

? "Elf" was partly filmed in New York without permits.

? Jim Carrey trained with a Navy SEAL to survive the Grinch costume.

? The snow in "Home Alone" was made from potato flakes.

The cottage from "The Holiday" is a real house in England.

FUN FACT QUICKFIRE: *Holiday Movie Trivia*

- Elf (2003) was partly filmed in New York without permits — some of the scenes of Buddy running through crowds were completely real.
- The Nightmare Before Christmas took over three years to make using stop-motion animation.
- The scarf from Harry Potter and the Philosopher's Stone Christmas scene sold at auction for about $12,000.

End-of-Day Wisdom

Behind every classic carol and beloved movie lies a story of luck, chaos, and a touch of magic. Some songs ended up in space, some flopped into fame - and one school gym became cinematic history.

You've completed Day 7 of your Toilet Advent Calendar.

Go ahead - hum Jingle Bells, quote Home Alone, and remember: Christmas classics were born from happy accidents.

DAY 8

Christmas Inventions & Firsts

Main Trivia #1: *The first electric Christmas lights*

Before electric bulbs twinkled on trees, Victorians decorated with candles - a beautiful but dangerous choice.

In 1882, Edward H. Johnson, an associate of Thomas Edison, decided to test a safer idea. He hand-wired 80 red, white, and blue bulbs and placed them on his Christmas tree in New York City.

Newspapers called it "a marvelous sight," though most people still couldn't afford electricity. Within two decades, the idea spread — by the 1920s, electric Christmas lights became a middle-class must-have, and candle-lit trees quietly retired.

💪 Christmas Table Flex:

"Electric Christmas lights were invented by Thomas Edison's assistant after almost burning down his house with candles. Innovation really is self-preservation."

TOTALLY USELESS RECORDS YOU DIDN'T ASK FOR:

In parts of Brussels, public toilets with a red icon are paid, while blue icon ones are free – so the right color decides whether you pay or pee for free.

The town of Regensburg in Germany set a Guinness World Record by organizing a parade of 897 Dachshunds, earning the title "Largest Dachshund Walk".

Mini Thought:

sometimes "Holiday spirit" just means not burning down your living room.

The world's first commercial Christmas card was created in 1843 by Sir Henry Cole – the same year Dickens published A Christmas Carol.

Cole commissioned artist John Callcott Horsley to design a card showing a family celebrating with wine and the words "A Merry Christmas and a Happy New Year to You." Some critics found it "immoral" because a child appeared to sip from a glass. Scandal or not, the cards sold out – and by the 1860s, the Christmas card industry was booming.

Today, more than a billion cards are still sent each year, though most end up as festive fridge decor or next year's gift tags.

💪 *Christmas Table Flex:*

"Victorians: inventors of the commercial Christmas card... and accidental festive scandals."

FUN FACT QUICKFIRE:
Christmas "Firsts" You Didn't Know

- The first recorded use of "Xmas" dates back to 1021, when monks used the Greek letter Chi (X) for Christ.
- The first Christmas song to hit #1 on Billboard was "The Chipmunk Song" in 1958.
- The first Christmas movie ever made was "Santa Claus" (1898), a silent British short lasting just over a minute.
- The first "ugly Christmas sweater" party took place in Vancouver in 2002 – now a worldwide phenomenon.

Bonus Fact Corner: Holiday Firsts & Surprising Origins

🎁 The first Christmas stamp was issued in Canada in 1898, though it wasn't officially meant for Christmas – it just said "XMAS 1898" and accidentally started a tradition.

🎁 The first artificial snow used in movies (including It's a Wonderful Life) was made from asbestos. Yes, the toxic kind.

🎁 The first televised Christmas speech by a British monarch was delivered by King George V in 1932 on BBC radio – the first TV broadcast came 25 years later.

🎁 The first Santa parade took place in Peoria, Illinois, in 1887, originally called "The Christmas Street Fair."

🎁 The first plastic Christmas tree was produced by a toilet-brush company (Addis Brush, 1937). It used the same bristles as their cleaning tools – festive and hygienic.

MINI QUIZ - CHRISTMAS FIRSTS EDITION
Which of these "firsts" actually happened?

A. The first electric Christmas lights were installed on a tree by Edison himself.

B. The first Christmas card caused outrage for showing a child drinking wine.

C. The first artificial tree was made of real pine dipped in wax.

End-of-Day Wisdom

From fiery trees to toilet-brush Christmas pines, history shows that holiday magic often starts with an accident, a spark, or a questionable idea.

DAY 9

Christmas Records & Extreme Festivities

Main Trivia #1: *The biggest community Christmas dinner*

Every year in London, the charity Crisis hosts one of the world's largest community Christmas meals for people experiencing homelessness. In 2019, over 9,000 guests were served a full festive dinner by more than 12,000 volunteers across multiple centers. Each meal includes roast turkey, vegetables, dessert, and even small gifts – plus access to showers, haircuts, and medical care. It's one of the biggest coordinated Christmas efforts on the planet – turning kindness into a logistical masterpiece.

💪 Christmas Table Flex:

"London's biggest Christmas miracle? 9,000 free dinners, 12,000 volunteers, and zero table fights."

TOTALLY USELESS RECORDS YOU DIDN'T ASK FOR:

In Brussels, Belgium, it is explicitly forbidden to urinate in public (on the street) – offenders risk fines of up to about €250 for public peeing.

Most toilet paper rolls balanced on the head: 46 rolls – achieved by James Rawlings (UK) on 29 September 2020, in Chinnor, UK.

Mini Thought: Who needs santa when you've got an army of volunteers with gravy boats?

In 2014, the Gay family from New York set a Guinness World Record for the most Christmas lights on a residential property –
a dazzling 601,736 bulbs covering their house, trees, and yard.
The setup used nearly 30 miles of wire, synchronized to Christmas music, and raised money for local charities.
Their record has since been beaten by Australian decorators with over 1.2 million lights, but the Gay family's epic display remains one of the most iconic holiday setups ever made.

Christmas Table Flex:

"The record for the most Christmas lights on a home is over 600,000. The neighbors probably moved."

Bonus Fact Corner: Records That Sleigh

The tallest snowman ever built stood 122 feet tall in Maine (2008). It was named "Olympia Snowe," after a U.S. senator.

The largest Secret Santa exchange took place online in 2020, with over 220,000 participants from 160 countries.

The fastest time to wrap a Christmas present is 9.38 seconds, achieved by Guinness record holder Sheena Wrigley from the UK.

The most Christmas sweaters worn at once was 260 people layered up in Ireland in 2019.

The largest gingerbread house was built in Texas, 2013 – it used 35 million calories worth of ingredients and even had space for Santa inside.

FUN FACT QUICKFIRE: *Holiday Excesses*

- The record for the largest gathering of Santas was set in India in 2014 – 18,112 people dressed as St. Nick.
- The longest Christmas cracker ever made was 207 feet long – about the size of a blue whale.
- The most expensive Christmas tree was decorated at a luxury hotel in Spain in 2019, worth $15 million.
- The largest snowball fight took place in Seattle in 2013, with over 7,600 participants.

MINI QUIZ - WORLD RECORDS EDITION
Which one of these records is real?

A. The largest Christmas cookie ever baked weighed over 500 kg.

B. The fastest carol singing marathon lasted 72 hours straight.

C. The biggest group of elves danced in the streets of Canada.

D. The longest Christmas dinner table stretched 600 meters.

End-of-Day Wisdom

Christmas brings out the best (and strangest) in us - from giant snowmen to homes brighter than the sun.

The records may sound absurd, but they all share one thing: people coming together for fun, generosity, and a touch of madness.

You've completed Day 9 of your Toilet Advent Calendar.

Tomorrow, we'll meet the true holiday heroes - the animals who accidentally stole Christmas.

DAY 10

Christmas Animals & Unexpected Heroes

Main Trivia #1: *Reindeer – the real deal behind Santa's team*

Santa's reindeer might be magical, but real reindeer are impressive enough on their own. They can see ultraviolet light, which helps them spot food and predators in Arctic darkness. Both males and females grow antlers – so Rudolph's team probably includes a lot of girls. Reindeer also have special noses that warm freezing air before it reaches their lungs and can run up to 50 mph. In winter, their eyes even change color – from gold in summer to deep blue – to adapt to the dim light of the polar night.

Christmas Table Flex:

"Reindeer can't actually fly, but they can see ultraviolet light. Which means Santa's sleigh must look insane to them."

TOTALLY USELESS RECORDS YOU DIDN'T ASK FOR:

In Singapore, failing to flush a public toilet is actually against the law. There are fines for not flushing in shared or public toilets.

Most candy canes in a beard: 200 candy canes - a festive beard-decoration feat where the record is 200 candy canes!

Mini Thought:

Turns out Rudolph's nose didn't need to glow - nature already gave reindeer all the cool upgrades.

Every December since 1947, the city of Oslo, Norway has sent a towering Christmas tree to London's Trafalgar Square.

It's a thank-you for Britain's support during World War II - and one of the longest-running international Christmas traditions.

The tree, usually a 50- to 60-year-old Norwegian spruce, is cut by hand, shipped across the North Sea, and decorated in traditional Norwegian style with vertical white lights.

Even when the 2021 tree caused controversy for looking "a bit sparse," Londoners still loved it - because the gesture, not the symmetry, is what counts.

Christmas Table Flex:

"In 1947, a group of war-weary sailors gifted Britain a Christmas tree. The tree became a yearly legend - and a symbol of peace."

Bonus Fact Corner: Holiday Animals You Didn't Expect

In Finland, horses play a big role - sleigh rides are a national Christmas pastime.

In Poland, families set an extra seat at the Christmas Eve table, sometimes for a stranger - but symbolically, it's also for a lost loved one or even a wandering animal.

In Iceland, cats have a darker side - the Yule Cat legend says it eats anyone who doesn't get new clothes for Christmas (good motivation to do laundry).

In Australia, Santa sometimes arrives on a surfboard pulled by kangaroos called "Six White Boomers."

In Ukraine, spiders are seen as lucky Christmas creatures - their webs are said to shimmer like silver in the morning light.

FUN FACT QUICKFIRE:
Animals and Christmas History

- The first live reindeer ever used in U.S. holiday parades appeared in New York in 1926.
- The Royal Mail once used donkeys to deliver Christmas cards to remote Scottish islands.
- WWI soldiers on the front lines shared rations with stray cats and dogs during the famous 1914 Christmas Truce.
- A penguin named Bagpipes from a New Zealand zoo once delivered Christmas gifts to children's wards dressed in a tiny Santa coat.

TRUE OR FALSE

? Reindeer noses turn red in winter because of extra blood flow.

The Yule Cat legend was invented in the 2000s as a joke.

? Norway sends a Christmas tree to London every ten years.

A penguin once delivered gifts to kids in New Zealand.

End-of-Day Wisdom

Animals have been part of Christmas stories for centuries - guiding sleighs, inspiring myths, and stealing the spotlight. Sometimes the magic of the season doesn't wear boots - it has fur, feathers, or antlers.

DAY 11

Christmas Rebels & Rule Breakers

Main Trivia #1: When Christmas was banned

In the 1600s, England's Puritan government under Oliver Cromwell banned Christmas celebrations.

They saw the holiday as a sinful, wasteful, and "papist" festival full of drunkenness and pagan symbols. Shops stayed open on December 25th, soldiers confiscated mince pies, and even singing carols could get you fined.

But people rebelled — they baked puddings in secret and decorated their homes anyway. When the monarchy returned in 1660, the ban was lifted, and the people of Britain celebrated like never before.

💪 Christmas Table Flex:

"In the 1600s, Christmas was banned in England. Yes, people once got fined for eating pie."

TOTALLY USELESS RECORDS YOU DIDN'T ASK FOR:

In some countries such as Turkey, Greece and Egypt you must throw used toilet paper into a bin instead of flushing it. Their plumbing systems can't handle flushed paper, so standard practice is to use a waste-bin.

Most socks worn on one foot simultaneously: 184 socks - achieved by Kamil Kulik in Wrocław, Poland, on 6 September 2016.

Mini Thought:

Once upon a time, Christmas was illegal. And you thought your boss was a Grinch.

After the 1959 revolution, Fidel Castro's government removed Christmas from the public calendar, declaring it a distraction from sugar production and socialist work goals.

For nearly three decades, December 25th was just another workday.

That changed in 1997, when Pope John Paul II planned a visit. Castro restored Christmas as a national holiday to honor the occasion – and the tradition has remained ever since.

Today, Cubans celebrate with midnight feasts, roast pork, and fireworks – proof that even politics can't keep the Christmas spirit down forever.

Ho ho ho!

💪 Christmas Table Flex:

"In Cuba, Christmas was gone for 29 years – then came back because the Pope asked nicely."

Bonus Fact Corner: Festive Rule Breakers 🎁

In Boston, USA, Christmas was banned from 1659 to 1681, and anyone caught celebrating had to pay a fine.

In Scotland, Christmas wasn't an official public holiday until 1958 – people worked as usual for almost 400 years.

In Japan, a department store once printed a Christmas ad showing Santa being crucified – it was quickly pulled after complaints.

In France (1951), Catholic youth groups burned an effigy of Santa Claus in public, claiming he distracted from the real meaning of Christmas.

In England (1647), mobs actually rioted in Canterbury after soldiers tore down their Christmas decorations – proving that even tinsel can start a revolution.

FUN FACT QUICKFIRE:
Christmas Controversies

- The Vatican Nativity scene of 2020 featured a ceramic astronaut and caused international confusion.
- In 1971, a man in Florida was fined for hanging Christmas lights shaped like swear words.
- In 1944, U.S. soldiers in WWII Germany celebrated Christmas in a bombed-out church – technically violating curfew, but no one stopped them.
- The first "anti-Christmas" movie, Santa Claus Conquers the Martians (1964), was so bad it's now a cult holiday classic.
- In 2010, a British town banned the word "Christmas" from public decorations to appear more "inclusive" – locals put it back up anyway.
- In 1958, Canada accidentally issued a Christmas stamp showing Santa without his hat – collectors went wild.
- In 2013, a Florida city removed its "Festivus pole" after residents turned it into a beer can sculpture.
- In 2005, a British school banned Christmas cards to "save the environment" – parents mailed twice as many anyway.

End-of-Day Wisdom

No matter how many times people have tried to cancel, control, or sanitize Christmas, it keeps finding its way back - louder, brighter, and with more pudding. You can ban the party, but you can't ban the joy.

DAY 12

Close Calls & Odd Emergencies

Main Trivia #1: *Fire in the White House*

In 1929, the White House Christmas tree lights short-circuited and started a small fire in the Blue Room.

President Herbert Hoover and his family were inside when staff noticed smoke.

Luckily, the fire was contained before it reached the branches.

It was the first Christmas that led to an official "fireproof wiring" rule for all government decorations.

💪 Christmas Table Flex:

"In 1929, a short circuit nearly ruined the president's Christmas – talk about a stressful holiday."

TOTALLY USELESS RECORDS YOU DIDN'T ASK FOR:

Most spoons balanced on the body: 96 spoons – Abolfazl Saber Mokhtari balanced 96 spoons on his body to set the current record.

A cat named Pugsley, a 2-year-old Maine Coon from Minnesota, broke the record for the longest tail on a living domestic cat - measuring 18.5 inches.

Mini Thought:

Turns out, even the White House couldn't handle too much holiday spirit.

In December 2009, Auckland Airport in New Zealand was evacuated after a suspicious package triggered a bomb alert.

The package turned out to be a homemade gingerbread house with a musical light box that malfunctioned and ticked like a timer.

Hundreds of passengers spent hours outside while the bomb squad investigated the sugary suspect.

Mini Thought:

Proof tHat even cookies can cause cHaos if you wire tHem wrong.

Christmas Table Flex:

"In 2009, a gingerbread gift caused a bomb scare in New Zealand – the sweetest false alarm in history."

FUN FACT QUICKFIRE:
Christmas Controversies

- In the UK more than 1 in 5 candle-fires each year occur in December.
- In Anchorage, Alaska, the famous pet reindeer Star was found wandering downtown after someone cut the lock to its pen.
- Official UK fire data show December remains the peak month for house-fires and insurance claims related to Christmas decorations.

Bonus Fact Corner: Real Holiday Emergencies

Wind vs. Wonder — In 2024, a massive 184-foot floating Christmas tree display near Rio de Janeiro collapsed during a storm, causing chaos at the waterfront.

Deck the Halls (Carefully) — Between 2007 and 2016, over 20,000 people in the U.S. ended up in ERs due to Christmas tree–related injuries.

Festive Fire Hazards — Austrian fire services reported hundreds of household fires each year caused by real Christmas trees and candles.

Tree Trouble in Belgium — In 2023, high winds toppled a giant Christmas tree at a market in Oudenaarde, leaving behind a very flattened festive scene.

TRUE OR FALSE

? The White House once had a Christmas tree fire while the president was inside.

Rio's floating Christmas tree once caught fire during a storm. **?**

? A German police call turned out to be caused by a sleeping hedgehog.

A man cooked his Christmas dinner with a space heater on purpose.

End-of-Day Wisdom

Christmas may bring chaos, but at least it's never boring. If nothing goes wrong, are you even doing it right?

DAY 13

Unusual Christmas Jobs & Holiday Hustles

Main Trivia #1: *The Business of Being Santa*

In the U.S. alone, there are over 30,000 professional Santas who train, certify, and audition for holiday jobs.

Some earn more than $20,000 in one season – if they have the perfect belly, beard, and background check.

Top-tier Santas attend "Santa schools," where they practice laugh techniques and reindeer trivia.

At one convention, attendees debated whether glitter in beards is "authentic" or "off-brand."

For many, the job isn't about cash but connection – being everyone's temporary grandpa for a month.

💪 Christmas Table Flex:

"In 1890, a Massachusetts store hired the first professional Santa – and the side hustle hasn't slowed down since."

TOTALLY USELESS RECORDS YOU DIDN'T ASK FOR:

Honey never spoils – jars found in ancient Egyptian tombs were still edible. It's basically the world's slowest-moving food trend.

Octopuses have three hearts and favorite nap spots. More hearts, more feelings... probably.

Mini Thought:

It's the only season where a fake beard and a belly can land you a five-figure paycheck.

In Japan, you can rent a "holiday companion" to join your family meal or pose in Christmas selfies.

Rates range from $60 to $200 an hour — more if you want the date to wear a Santa hat.

Meanwhile, professional gift wrappers work in malls worldwide, charging extra for bows, ribbons, or "emotional damage repair."

In 2019, one New York wrapper boasted she could fold anything, including a kayak and a cat tree.

For some, holiday hustle means love by the hour; for others, precision tape application.

💪 Christmas Table Flex:

"In Japan, you can literally rent a date for Christmas dinner — because nothing says festive like paying someone to meet your parents."

Bonus Fact Corner: Odd Jobs of the Holiday Season

Toy companies hire "play-testers" to check the durability and safety of toys before the Christmas rush.

The Canada Post replies to over a million letters addressed to Santa each year.

In the UK there was once a real seasonal job advertisement for a "Christmas cracker joke writer".

In Finnish Lapland you can find seasonal jobs as reindeer guides or handlers working with visitors around Christmas in the Santa Claus Village, Rovaniemi.

One luxury hotel decorator job pays thousands of dollars per project to install Christmas tree displays, lights and decorations in high-end venues.

FUN FACT QUICKFIRE:
Christmas Side Gigs Edition

- There's an annual "Santa School" in Michigan – founded in 1937.
- Japan's rent-a-family industry spikes 30% in December.
- In the U.S., approximately 3 billion Christmas cards are sent each year.
- Norway even offers Santa beard insurance – in case of fake-fur accidents.

TRUE OR FALSE

There's a professional "turkey taste tester" job in the UK.

The world's most expensive Santa suit cost over $10,000.

Finland trains its mall Santas at a national Santa academy.

The first paid Santa appearance was in a New York store in 1890.

End-of-Day Wisdom

Not everyone gets a silent night - some get overtime pay and glitter in awkward places. Whether it's wrapping, posing, or pretending, these jobs remind us that Christmas runs on more than magic — it runs on hustle.

DAY 14

The Science of Christmas

Main Trivia #1: *The Physics of Christmas Lights*

A single strand of 100 traditional bulbs uses about 40 watts of power, while the same number of LEDs uses less than 5. If every household in the U.S. switched to LEDs, it could save enough energy to power 200,000 homes for a year. In 2010, NASA even analyzed how Christmas lights changed the brightness of entire cities seen from space. Their findings showed urban areas glowing up to 20% –50% brighter during the holidays, especially in suburbs.

It turns out holiday cheer is literally visible from orbit – glowing proof that sentimentality burns bright and costs extra.

Christmas Table Flex:

"Satellite data show some cities glow 20–50% brighter during December holidays - even space can tell we overdid the lights."

TOTALLY USELESS RECORDS YOU DIDN'T ASK FOR:

Sharks are older than trees – over 400 million years.
They're the original hipsters of Earth.

Bananas are berries, but strawberries aren't.
Botany refuses to make sense on purpose.

Mini Thought:

Every December, millions of trees are decorated, billions of lights are plugged in - and one poor physicist somewhere calculates the wattage.

Scientists know that the "Christmas smell" is a cocktail of organic compounds – from vanillin in cookies to α-pinene in pine trees and eugenol in cloves.

These molecules trigger the limbic system, the brain's emotional center, which is why gingerbread feels like therapy and mulled wine like a hug.

One study found that just smelling cinnamon can increase alertness by 25%.

So yes, your brain gets a literal buzz from baked goods – no caffeine required.

Christmas Table Flex:

"The smell of Christmas cookies isn't magic – it's chemistry armed with butter and nostalgia."

FUN FACT QUICKFIRE:
Scientific Christmas Edition

- Astronauts on Apollo 8 read from Genesis while orbiting the Moon on Christmas Eve 1968.
- A 2019 study found that poorly wrapped gifts create lower expectations and increase recipient satisfaction.
- The first artificial Christmas trees were made from dyed goose feathers in late 19th-century Germany.
- NORAD's Santa Tracker began in 1955 after a child misdialed a phone number printed in a Sears ad.

Bonus Fact Corner: Holiday Science

The scent of real Christmas trees contains natural oils called phytoncides, which have been shown to reduce stress and boost your mood.

Reindeer noses really turn red due to a dense network of blood vessels that help regulate temperature in freezing air.

Snow appears white because its ice crystals scatter all wavelengths of visible light.

The world's largest recorded snowflake measured 15 inches wide in Fort Keogh, Montana, 1887.

Poinsettias aren't actually very poisonous – a child would have to eat hundreds of leaves to get sick.

TRUE OR FALSE

The "smell of snow" comes from ozone released in cold air.

Eating gingerbread can improve your reaction time.

Christmas tree needles can conduct small amounts of electricity.

NASA once tracked Santa using a radar glitch.

End-of-Day Wisdom

Turns out, holiday magic is just science in a glittery hat. From glowing lights to fizzy drinks and feel-good smells - it's chemistry, physics, and a sprinkle of emotional chaos. And honestly? We love to see it.

✴ DAY 15 ✴

Christmas in Space

Main Trivia #1: *The First Christmas Among the Stars*

On December 24, 1968, Apollo 8 astronauts Frank Borman, Jim Lovell and Bill Anders became the first humans to celebrate Christmas in space.

They read from Genesis while broadcasting live to Earth, their voices reaching over a billion people.

Anders took the famous "Earthrise" photo — a reminder that the most beautiful ornament that Christmas was our planet itself.

No tree, no gifts, just three men floating in silence above a blue and white world.

💪 *Christmas Table Flex:*

"In 1968, the Apollo 8 crew spent Christmas orbiting the Moon — and accidentally sent the most poetic holiday card in history."

TOTALLY USELESS RECORDS YOU DIDN'T ASK FOR:

Butterflies taste with their feet. So walking through a buffet must be wild.

Some turtles can breathe through their butts. Nature truly committed to efficiency.

Mini Thought:

Turns out the best view of Christmas Lights is from the moon.

Astronauts on the International Space Station have celebrated Christmas every year since 2000.

They decorate with tiny Velcro trees, play holiday music, and share vacuum-sealed turkey and cranberry sauce.

In 2012, Canadian astronaut Chris Hadfield recorded a version of "Space Oddity" that became an instant classic back on Earth.

Even in zero gravity, they exchange small gifts and messages from home - proof that tradition survives even without gravity.

💪 Christmas Table Flex:

"In 2000, the crew of the International Space Station hung stockings - then taped them down so they wouldn't float away."

Bonus Fact Corner: Christmas in Space

Apollo 8 was the first mission to broadcast a live Christmas message from space in 1968.

Skylab astronauts made a homemade Christmas tree from food containers in 1973.

The first Christmas meal in space included turkey and fruitcake (Apollo 8 menu archives).

The ISS crew has celebrated Christmas every year since 2000.

Astronauts often display family photos and paper decorations that float freely around the module.

FUN FACT QUICKFIRE:
Space Holiday Edition

- Astronauts see about 16 sunrises on Christmas Day aboard the ISS.
- Chris Hadfield played a guitar made on Earth for his 2012 holiday song.
- The ISS orbits Earth every 90 minutes — so they get a new "Christmas Eve" roughly 16 times.
- Apollo 17 (1972) left a tiny ceramic angel figurine on the Moon.

TRUE OR FALSE

? Apollo 8 astronauts brought a small Bible to space.

No Christmas music has ever been played in space. ?

? The first Christmas tree in orbit was made of wires and Velcro.

Santa has been officially tracked by NORAD since the 1950s.

End-of-Day Wisdom

EVEN FAR BEYOND EARTH'S ATMOSPHERE, HUMANS FIND A WAY TO MAKE THE UNIVERSE FEEL A LITTLE LIKE HOME.

CHRISTMAS IN SPACE PROVES THAT TRADITION ISN'T BOUND BY GRAVITY — ONLY BY IMAGINATION.

DAY 16

Gift Fails & Awkward Presents

Main Trivia #1: *The Royal Gift Game*

Each Christmas Eve at Sandringham, the British royal family exchange joke gifts instead of luxuries.

It is reported that Princess Anne once gave her brother a white-leather toilet seat, and Prince Harry once presented the Queen with a singing fish plaque.

The tradition likely dates back decades and is meant to keep the festivities light-hearted and free of formality.

Even royalty knows that nothing breaks etiquette like a novelty gift and a good laugh.

Christmas Table Flex:

"The British royal family open their presents on Christmas Eve – and the cheaper the gift, the bigger the laugh."

TOTALLY USELESS RECORDS YOU DIDN'T ASK FOR:

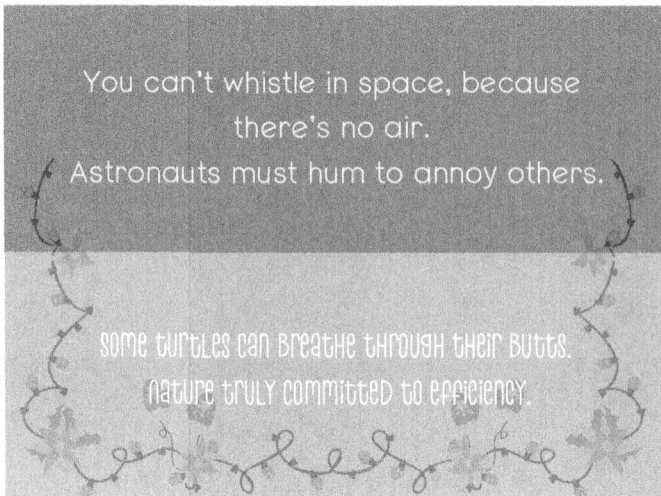

You can't whistle in space, because there's no air.
Astronauts must hum to annoy others.

Some turtles can breathe through their butts.
Nature truly committed to efficiency.

Mini Thought:

Sometimes the best presents are the ones you can't take too seriously.

Every year, online resale platforms like eBay and Vinted see a sharp spike in listings starting on Boxing Day.

According to retail analysts, returns and resales form a major part of the post-holiday economy.

Studies show that roughly one-third of people have re-gifted something they received, and many more admit to considering it.

A study by Finder.com found that the average person receives about $70 worth of unwanted gifts each Christmas.

Retail analytics show that nearly 10% of all holiday purchases end up being returned before New Year's Eve.

Turns out the season of giving also keeps the cycle of re-giving alive.

💪 *Christmas Table Flex:*

"After Christmas Day, millions of unwanted gifts quietly find their way to online marketplaces – some before the leftovers are cold."

FUN FACT QUICKFIRE: *Gift Edition*

- The first commercial gift-wrapping paper was created by the Hall Brothers in 1917 – founders of Hallmark.
- In Japan, beautifully wrapping a gift is crucial – the act itself shows respect and appreciation.
- Gift cards generate billions in unused balances each year.
- The average American spends around 15 hours shopping for Christmas presents.
- In the UK, 58% of adults say they've received a Christmas gift they don't like – that's about 31 million people.

Bonus Fact Corner: Records That Sleigh

❄ The royal family open their presents on Christmas Eve, following a German tradition.

❄ Retail returns peak on December 26, the day after Christmas.

❄ Surveys show that around 35% of people admit to re-gifting a present at least once.

❄ Gift cards are among the most commonly exchanged and returned items.

❄ Minimal-waste movements in Scandinavia encourage giving experiences instead of objects.

MINI QUIZ - GIFT GONE WRONG EDITION

1. WHEN DO THE BRITISH ROYALS OPEN THEIR CHRISTMAS PRESENTS?

a) Christmas morning   b) Christmas Eve   c) New Year's Day

2. WHICH ITEM HAS BEEN REPORTED AS A ROYAL GAG GIFT?

a) Toilet seat   b) Crown cleaner   c) Fake diamond slippers

3. WHEN DO RETAILERS SEE THE HIGHEST VOLUME OF RETURNS?

a) December 26   b) December 31   c) January 10

4. WHICH COUNTRY HAS INFLUENCED THE ROYAL FAMILY'S CHRISTMAS GIFT TRADITION?

a) France   b) Germany   c) Italy

End-of-Day Wisdom

Whether it's a toilet seat or a tie, what matters is the thought - and maybe the receipt. Even awkward presents prove that someone, somewhere, was thinking of you.

Festive Food Fiascos

Main Trivia #1: *Dessert on fire – a very British tradition*

The British Christmas pudding is a dense, fruit-packed dessert soaked in brandy and proudly set on fire before serving. The dramatic blue flame is meant to symbolize Christ's light, but for many families, it mostly symbolizes a yearly panic about setting off the smoke alarm. Each December, the London Fire Brigade issues reminders to warm the brandy gently before lighting it, warning that splashing cold alcohol over a hot pudding can ignite tablecloths or sleeves. Despite the risks, the flaming pudding remains a beloved spectacle that marks the finale of Christmas dinner. It's a culinary tradition equal parts faith, festivity, and fire hazard.

💪 Christmas Table Flex:

"In Britain, the only dessert that comes with its own fire hazard is the Christmas pudding – it's tradition to set it alight with brandy."

TOTALLY USELESS RECORDS YOU DIDN'T ASK FOR

Squirrels forget about 80% of the nuts they bury.
Accidentally becoming the world's best gardeners.

Cows have best friends and get stressed when separated. Yes, even cows need emotional support.

Mini Thought:

A little brandy can lift the mood - and the flames, if you're careless.

In late 2011, Norway experienced a national "butter crisis" that became an international headline. A wet summer had reduced milk production, cutting butter supplies just as Norwegians began their annual Christmas baking season. Demand skyrocketed after a popular high-fat diet trend encouraged people to cook with real butter instead of margarine. Prices soared on the black market — a single packet cost up to 300 kroner (about $50) — and people drove across borders to Denmark and Sweden to stock up. The government finally relaxed import restrictions to stabilize supplies, but by then the damage to cookie morale was done. It was a humbling reminder that even the happiest holidays can crumble without fat.

BUTTER

Christmas Table Flex:

"In 2011, Norway's butter shelves went bare before Christmas — a crisis that made pastry lovers weep into their dry cookies."

Bonus Fact Corner: Festive Food Facts

Japan's Christmas fried-chicken tradition is so popular that KFC manages preorders and has seen stores run out during peak days.

The largest gingerbread house on record was built in Bryan, Texas, in 2013, certified by Guinness World Records.

In Iceland, fermented skate is traditionally eaten on Þorláksmessa, December 23, right before Christmas.

UK authorities publish Christmas food-safety guidance each year, including detailed advice on thawing and cooking turkey.

FUN FACT QUICKFIRE:
Holiday Food Edition

- Guinness certifies the 2013 Texas gingerbread house as the largest ever.
- Norway's 2011 butter crisis disrupted Christmas baking nationwide.
- KFC at Christmas in Japan generates such demand that long lines and sell-outs have been documented.
- UK fire services issue Christmas cooking safety tips to prevent kitchen fires.

MINI QUIZ - FESTIVE FEAST EDITION

1. WHICH DESSERT IS TRADITIONALLY FLAMBÉED WITH BRANDY IN THE UK?

a) Panettone   b) Christmas pudding   c) Fruitcake

2. WHICH COUNTRY FACED A BUTTER SHORTAGE DURING THE 2011 CHRISTMAS SEASON?

a) Sweden   b) Norway   c) Denmark

3. WHERE WAS THE GUINNESS-CERTIFIED LARGEST GINGERBREAD HOUSE BUILT IN 2013?

a) Munich   b) Bryan, Texas   c) Copenhagen

4. WHICH FAST-FOOD BRAND IS TIED TO CHRISTMAS DINNER TRADITIONS IN JAPAN?

a) McDonald's   b) KFC   c) Domino's

End-of-Day Wisdom

Holiday cooking proves one thing - perfection isn't on the menu.
Between burnt puddings, late turkeys, and creative substitutions, it's the laughter that actually gets served hot.

Lost & Found Christmases

Main Trivia #1: *The Wedding Ring Under the Tree*

In 2010, a man visiting a Christmas tree farm in Newport, Virginia lost his wedding ring while choosing a tree. Staff kept a handwritten note about it posted on their bulletin board, and it stayed there as the farm changed owners. Fifteen years later, the new owners found the ring while working the land, matched it to the old note and returned it to its owner. The ring had vanished for over a decade, only to turn up exactly where the season started: under the trees.

Christmas Table Flex:

"A Virginia tree farm found a long-lost wedding ring after 15 years in the soil. Even jewelry needs a break from commitment."

TOTALLY USELESS RECORDS YOU DIDN'T ASK FOR:

Hummingbirds are the only birds that can fly backward.
They'd be great at parallel parking.

onions have more DNA than Humans.
WHICH explains absolutely nothing.

Mini Thought:

some things get lost... and some just hide on purpose.

In 2020, a woman in New Jersey received a package addressed to her long-deceased mother. Inside was a Christmas present from 1983 – a vinyl record that her uncle had mailed but never realized went missing.
The USPS had just found it in a forgotten corner of a distribution center – 37 years later. Still sealed. Still playable.
The woman called it "a message from my mom and uncle, straight out of time."

🦾 Christmas Table Flex:

"In 1983, a Christmas gift vanished in the mail. In 2020, it finally showed up. Turns out Santa just had a backlog."

Bonus Fact Corner: Real-Life Lost & Found Christmases

In 2014, a woman in Canada found her grandmother's antique Christmas ornament inside a box of donations at a secondhand shop 1,000 km away – it had been accidentally given away years earlier.

A WWII-era Christmas card addressed to a soldier in France was delivered to his daughter in 2015 – 70 years late, but just in time for her first Christmas without him.

In 2022, a British woman received a Christmas postcard originally mailed in 1919. It had vanished for 103 years.

One man found his childhood stocking in a thrift store in 2018, still with his name stitched on – his family had lost it during a move in the '90s.

FUN FACT QUICKFIRE: *Lost & Found Edition*

- The oldest Santa letter ever found dates back to 1898 and is archived in Dublin, Ireland.
- The most delayed Christmas card was delivered 93 years after it was sent – in 2011, in the UK.
- USPS processes over 15 million letters to Santa each year – some addressed simply as "North Pole."
- In 2020, a donation center in Arizona found $5,000 tucked into an old Christmas cookie tin.
- In 2021, a letter to Santa sent from Argentina was found 13,000 km away on a beach in France – still sealed and perfectly intact.

MINI QUIZ - LOST & FOUND EDITION
Which of these really happened?

A. A Christmas card from 1919 was delivered in 2022

B. A gingerbread house was found inside a wall

C. A reindeer returned a lost scarf

D. A Christmas tree grew inside a chimney

End-of-Day Wisdom

Christmas has a funny way of resurfacing - whether it's through a letter in a chimney, a dusty old ornament, or a package 37 years late. The things we think are gone sometimes just need time to find their way back.

You've made it through Day 18 of your Toilet Advent Calendar - and now you know: some stories are worth the wait.

DAY 19

Winter Oddities Around the World

Main Trivia #1: *The Night of the Radishes*

Every December 23rd in Oaxaca, Mexico, thousands gather not for gifts or snow – but for vegetables.

La Noche de los Rábanos (The Night of the Radishes) is a local holiday where artisans carve enormous radishes into elaborate scenes: nativity displays, animals, dancers – all made from oversized root vegetables. The tradition began in the 1800s, when farmers decorated radishes to attract customers at Christmas markets. Today it's a full-blown competition with cash prizes and crowds of over 20,000.These radishes aren't for eating – they're bred to grow big and weird just for the show.

💪 Christmas Table Flex:

"Some countries carve radishes into art, others dive into frozen lakes for fun. Let's just agree that winter makes us all weird."

TOTALLY USELESS RECORDS YOU DIDN'T ASK FOR

The oldest known fish lived around 500 years.
Imagine trying to remember where you parked your fins.

One jellyfish species can rejuvenate itself and is technically immortal.
It ignores every skincare commercial ever.

Mini Thought:

not all Christmas stars are shiny - some are spicy and carved with a knife.

Not all winter oddities involve holidays. Some are just nature – or humans – showing off.

- Ice pancakes are natural, round ice formations that appear on rivers in cold climates like Estonia, Scotland, and parts of the U.S. They form when slushy ice starts rotating in eddies – like nature's attempt at a frozen breakfast.
- In Sweden and Norway, people regularly swim in holes cut into frozen lakes – on purpose. Ice swimming is often followed by sauna time, and it's believed to boost circulation, immunity, and shock your soul back into your body.
- Meanwhile, Norway's Ice Music Festival features instruments made entirely from ice – drums, horns, even violins – carved from blocks of glacial ice and played under the open sky. The concerts melt slightly during performance, adding a touch of existential drama to every note.

FUN FACT QUICKFIRE: *Frozen & Festive Edition*

- Antarctica has hosted multiple Christmas parties. Research station crews celebrate the holidays with surprising flair – think decorated labs, potluck dinners, and yes, penguin-themed karaoke. Some stations even broadcast holiday radio shows or perform skits, proving that isolation + snow + scientists = chaotic holiday genius.
- Ice pancakes can reach up to 1 meter wide.
- The coldest New Year's swim on record happened at −23°C in Siberia.
- One Canadian man once skated 30 km on a frozen lake in a Santa suit – just to deliver cookies.

- The world's only Ice Hotel (in Sweden) has to be rebuilt every year from scratch — and yes, the beds are made of ice.

Bonus Fact Corner:
Chilly Delights from Around the World

In Finland, there's a tradition called "polar bear dipping" on New Year's — a plunge into icy water while dressed as Santa.

In Japan, monks at the Saidai-ji Eyo Hadaka Matsuri pour cold water on themselves in purifying winter rituals (barely dressed, but deeply committed).

In South Korea, people compete in an annual ice-fishing festival, cutting holes in frozen rivers to catch trout — some even do it bare-handed.

In Canada, the town of Yellowknife celebrates Snowking Festival inside a castle made of snow and ice — with concerts, slides, and snowball fights.

In Russia, Orthodox Epiphany bathers dive into cross-shaped ice holes blessed by priests, shouting prayers while submerged.

In Estonia, people sit in hot saunas on Christmas Eve... and then run outside to roll in the snow. It's less about cleanliness and more about "waking up the soul".

End-of-Day Wisdom

From radish sculptures to frozen orchestras and icy dips in near-death temperatures, winter traditions prove one thing: cold weather doesn't freeze creativity - it just makes it shiver in style. You've made it through Day 19 of your toilet advent calendar. Reward yourself with something warm. Like socks. Or dignity.

DAY 20

Santa Scandals & Fake Clauses

Main Trivia #1: *Santa behind bars*

Every year, someone in a Santa suit gets arrested – usually for public drunkenness, trespassing, or causing scenes that land them on the "naughty" list.

Top examples:

- UK, 2013: Banned from a shopping centre for moonwalking near escalators, causing chaos.
- USA, 2014: Escorted out of a mall for taking selfies with strangers' kids.
- Germany, 2017: Found passed out in a sleigh display, half-eaten bratwurst in hand.

Even Santa needs better decision-making after spiked eggnog.

💪 Christmas Table Flex:

"There are people who've been arrested while dressed as Santa. One of them moonwalked into mall security history."

TOTALLY USELESS RECORDS YOU DIDN'T ASK FOR

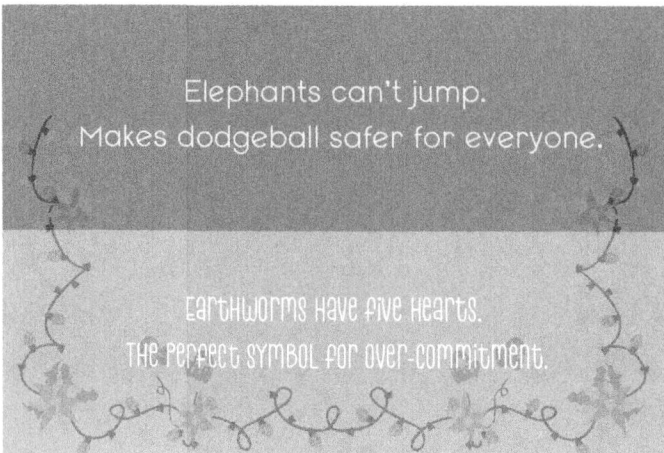

Elephants can't jump.
Makes dodgeball safer for everyone.

Earthworms have five hearts.
The perfect symbol for over-commitment.

Mini Thought:

Turns out, the naughty list has real consequences.

Not all kids' letters to Santa reach the North Pole. Some end up in surprising places:

- Florida, 2020: 400 letters were rerouted to a plumbing company on "North Pole Drive." The plumbers sent candy canes in response.
- UK, 2012: A chip shop got a stack of Santa letters and stuck them on the window, trading cod for kindness.
- USA: The USPS yearly gets letters addressed to "Santa Claws," "Satan Claus," and even "Santa Banana." They still deliver them.

Postal magic has a sense of humor.

Christmas Table Flex:

"Some Santa letters end up at the North Pole. Others go to plumbers, chippies, or 'Santa Banana' - and still get answered."

FUN FACT QUICKFIRE:
Santa & Scandal Edition

- The Guinness World Record for most Santas in one place is 18,112 (Portugal, 2008).
- In 2015, a woman sued a mall Santa for giving her child "a disappointing hug."
- The UK once had a hotline to report "naughty Santas" at office parties.
- In Tokyo, "Silent Santas" deliver gifts in nursing homes without saying a word – by tradition.
- There's a real event in Alaska called the "Santa Summit" – where impersonators meet to swap tips and beards.

Bonus Fact Corner: Real Santa Mayhem

✄ In Austria, police stopped a suspicious vehicle packed with wrapped boxes. The driver, dressed as Santa, was delivering illegal fireworks as "presents."

✄ In Texas, a man in a Santa costume got stuck in a chimney during a charity stunt and had to be rescued by firefighters – who were not amused.

✄ In Canada, a group of 20 Santas was kicked out of a bar for trying to pay only in candy canes and singing "Jingle Bells" at full volume.

✄ In Ireland, a Santa parachute jump went wrong when he landed on a golf course mid-tournament and was chased off by angry golfers.

✄ In New York, an actor playing Santa got stuck on a float during a Christmas parade and had to shout holiday greetings for 45 minutes while mechanics fixed the wheels.

MINI QUIZ - SANTA OR SCAMMER?
Which of these actually happened?

A. A mall Santa got sued for smelling like garlic and onions.

B. A Santa parachuted onto a golf course and was chased off by golfers.

C. 12 mall Santas were arrested for starting a snowball fight in a bank.

End-of-Day Wisdom

The world's full of fake clauses, naughty elves, and questionable Kris Kringles - but somehow, the magic still works. Maybe that's the real holiday miracle. You've survived Day 20 of your toilet advent calendar. No mugshots required.

DAY 21

Tech & Christmas Innovations

Main Trivia #1: *How Christmas got plugged in*

In 1882, Edward H. Johnson – an associate of Thomas Edison – hand-wired 80 red, white, and blue bulbs around his Christmas tree. People thought it was either genius... or witchcraft. The lights blinked. The tree spun.

Newspapers called it "a technological marvel." His kids just called it Christmas.

At the time, a string of electric lights cost more than most people earned in a week. Only the rich could afford them – and they often hired watchmen to guard the cables from curious guests.

Christmas Table Flex:

"The first electric Christmas lights were so expensive they had to be guarded. Literal festive security detail."

TOTALLY USELESS RECORDS YOU DIDN'T ASK FOR:

Pineapples grow on the ground, not on trees.
So tropical vibes, zero effort.

In space, your spine can stretch by up to 5 cm. The universe gives you free height, no gym required.

Mini Thought:

From candles to LEDs - and still someone always says "you missed a spot."

Technology didn't just light up trees – it rewired the holidays.

- The first e-card was sent in 1994. It took 8 minutes to load and played a MIDI version of "Jingle Bells."
- Google Trends tracks global searches like "last-minute gift" or "why is my turkey purple." The data peak? December 23rd.
- 3D printers now create custom ornaments, cookie cutters, and yes – life-sized Nutcrackers.
- In Japan, robot Santas have been used to greet shoppers and deliver presents in malls. Some even dance.

And yes – AI now writes Christmas poems, love letters, and questionable dinner menus. (You've been warned.)

Christmas Table Flex:

"In Japan, robot Santas deliver gifts. In the West, AI writes breakup letters on festive stationery. Happy holidays!"

Bonus Fact Corner: Christmas Tech Timeline

1882 – First electric tree lights

1947 – First recorded use of fake snow made from soap flakes

1955 – NORAD accidentally starts tracking "Santa" after a misprinted phone number

1999 – Amazon introduces Christmas gift wrap option

2020 – Zoom Christmas dinners become a thing (and a meme)

2023 – A viral TikTok filter gave everyone matching ugly sweaters.

FUN FACT QUICKFIRE: *Festive Tech Bites*

- The average American plugs in 7+ devices during the holidays (mostly lights, speakers, and stress).
- The first Christmas-themed emoji (like 🎅 and 🎄) became officially part of the global emoji set in 2010 with Unicode 6.0. However, festive icons had already appeared in earlier messaging apps long before that.
- In December 2022, U.S. retailer Walmart launched a drone delivery service in the Tampa Bay area, offering orders by drone for eligible customers as part of its seasonal push.
- According to a 2022 survey, three-quarters (73%) of holiday purchases across all generations are researched online beforehand.

TRUE OR FALSE

? The first electric Christmas tree lights were powered by a car battery.

AI once wrote a Christmas song that accidentally became a funeral jingle.

? The NORAD Santa Tracker started because of a wrong phone number.

3D printers have been used to make edible Christmas cookies.

End-of-Day Wisdom

THE TOOLS MAY CHANGE - FROM BLINKING BULBS TO BLINKING SCREENS - BUT THE POINT STAYS THE SAME: CONNECTION, CELEBRATION, AND SLIGHTLY TOO MANY EXTENSION CORDS.

YOU'VE MADE IT THROUGH DAY 21 OF YOUR TOILET ADVENT CALENDAR. NO NEED TO UPDATE YOUR FIRMWARE.

DAY 22

Pets, Animals & Holiday Mayhem

Main Trivia #1: *Fur-tive Christmas Crimes*

You spend hours decorating... and your pet destroys it in 30 seconds.

- A German Shepherd named Athena disappeared on December 15 and rang her family's doorbell on Christmas Eve.
- In 2020, a New York cat knocked over a candle and started a fire – the fire department featured her in a safety post.
- A UK retriever named Rollo went viral for unwrapping every gift under the tree – even the ones not his.

The holidays may be for humans – but pets have their own plans.

💪 Christmas Table Flex:

"It's not officially Christmas until something furry knocks over something glass."

TOTALLY USELESS RECORDS YOU DIDN'T ASK FOR

Ants don't sleep – they micro-rest. Basically tiny caffeine addicts.

Owls have eye tubes instead of eyeballs. Nature gave them built-in binoculars.

Mini Thought:

Alexa, stop the dog from ordering 12 pounds of beef jerky.

All over the world, animals sneak into Christmas – not just into your tree.

- In Iceland, kids leave food out for the mythical Yule Cat, said to eat those who don't get new clothes for Christmas. Motivation level: extreme.
- At Adelaide Zoo and Monarto Safari Park in Australia, animals enjoy a "Santa Paws" Christmas event every year–receiving decorated presents and treats unlike any human gift-exchange.
- In the U.S., malls now offer "Pet Santa" photo ops – because humans aren't the only ones who need proof they met the big guy.
- In Venezuela, some attend holiday mass with their pets to get them blessed – and it's not just dogs. Parrots and turtles welcome.

Animals may not understand Christmas, but they still end up in the family album.

Mini Thought:
OF COURSE I DRESSED MY DOG LIKE SANTA. HE DELIVERS JOY AND SHEDS EVERYWHERE.

FUN FACT QUICKFIRE: *Pet Edition*

- In Japan, Christmas cat costumes sell out weeks before the holidays.
- In the U.S., 1 in 3 pet owners buy their animal a holiday gift.
- Dogs can see Christmas lights – just mostly the blue and yellow ones.
- Some shelters let you "borrow" a dog for a Christmas walk.
- Guinea pigs in Santa hats? A whole online calendar genre.

Bonus Fact Corner: Furry, Fiery & Festive

In Canada, a deer was spotted with its antlers entangled in Christmas lights in Alberta.

In Sweden, the giant straw Gävle Goat ("julbocken") has become famous for being erected annually and repeatedly vandalised (especially by fire).

Popular Christmas-themed pet names in the U.S. and elsewhere include "Tinsel", "Ginger", "Snowball" among many festive-inspired suggestions.

During the holiday season, many "Pet Santa" photo-events take place in malls and animal shelters, giving pets their own Santa-moment. (Commonly reported in U.S. seasonal promotions.)

TRUE OR FALSE

? Some towns in the U.S. host "Santa Paws" events where pets take photos with Santa.

In the Czech Republic, people organize nativity church services for their hamsters. **?**

? A parrot once sang "Jingle Bells" live on radio and then cursed at the host.

Cats are biologically drawn to Christmas trees due to the smell of pine sap.

End-of-Day Wisdom

If your pet knocked over the tree, chewed the tinsel, and unwrapped a present, congratulations - you're doing Christmas right.

DAY 23

Christmas Around the Clock!

Main Trivia #1: *Christmas Starts...*

From BBQs in New Zealand to midnight mass in Bethlehem, time zones turn Christmas into a 24-hour world tour.

- Kiribati and New Zealand celebrate first – while most of the world is still asleep.
- In Alaska, Santa sometimes arrives by dog sled during parades and winter events.
- Orthodox countries like Russia or Serbia celebrate on January 7th.
- In Bethlehem, midnight mass at the Church of the Nativity is broadcast worldwide.

Wherever you are, the clock always says "Christmas" somewhere.

💪 Christmas Table Flex:

"In New Zealand, Christmas happens in shorts, not sweaters. Santa swaps cookies for sunscreen."

TOTALLY USELESS RECORDS YOU DIDN'T ASK FOR:

Male seahorses give birth.
Finally, someone else carries the baby.

cashews grow outside of the fruit.
they look like nature forgot how to attach them.

Mini Thought:

one planet. dozens of time zones. one very confused santa.

Not everyone dreams of a white Christmas. For some, the holiday season means flip-flops, heatwaves, and barbecued turkey.

- In Australia, Christmas falls in the middle of summer — many people spend it at the beach or having a grill party in the backyard.
- In South Africa, it's common to eat cold meat and salads to avoid using the oven in the heat.
- In Argentina, fireworks are a big Christmas Eve tradition — even though it's often 30°C outside.
- And in Brazil, Santa is sometimes spotted in shopping malls wearing shorts and sunglasses. He adapts.

Christmas Table Flex:

"Santa in flip-flops is still Santa - just slightly sweatier."

Bonus Fact Corner: Festive Facts from Far Away

In Samoa and Tonga, Christmas is celebrated up to 23 hours before Hawaii, thanks to the International Date Line.

Midnight Mass in Bethlehem is led by the Latin Patriarch of Jerusalem and attended by global dignitaries.

In Japan, Christmas Eve is treated like Valentine's Day — complete with KFC dinners and romantic dates.

In Mexico, Christmas punch (ponche navideño) includes tejocote fruit, sugar cane, cinnamon, and sometimes… chili.

FUN FACT QUICKFIRE:
Global Time Zone Chaos Edition

- You can technically celebrate Christmas 27 times if you travel fast enough through time zones.
- In Finland, many people visit cemeteries on Christmas Eve to light candles for loved ones.
- Christmas is a national holiday in India, despite Christians being a minority.
- Midnight Mass in Bethlehem is attended by both tourists and local Christians from across the region.
- Some U.S. states, like Hawaii, celebrate Christmas last due to their time zone.

TRUE OR FALSE

In Samoa, Christmas happens before it does in Australia.

In Greece, Orthodox Christmas is celebrated only on January 7th.

You could spend Christmas morning in New Zealand and Christmas night in Hawaii – on the same date.

Bethlehem celebrates Christmas with a live camel parade through the streets.

End-of-Day Wisdom

Time is just a suggestion. Christmas arrives when you're ready (or when Santa does).

DAY 24

The Magic of Small Traditions 🎁

Main Trivia #1: *Small Traditions, Big Feelings*

Not every tradition involves fireworks, camels, or synchronized light shows. Sometimes, it's about a shared cookie recipe, an awkward photo in matching pajamas, or one specific ornament that has to go on the tree first.

- In many families, the same old Christmas decorations are used year after year – even if half are broken, and one smells like the attic.
- Some households write a letter to their "future selves" every year and read the previous one on Christmas Eve.
- In Norway, families often watch the same Czech fairy tale film, Three Wishes for Cinderella, every Christmas – it's aired annually since the 70s.
- In some German homes, the "Weihnachtsgurke" – a glass pickle ornament – is hidden in the tree, and the first person to find it gets an extra gift or bragging rights.

Tiny traditions, lasting memories.

💪 Christmas Table Flex:

"We don't need fancy traditions. We've got our own weird little ones - and that's what makes them perfect."

TOTALLY USELESS RECORDS YOU DIDN'T ASK FOR:

Water striders can walk on water. They're the tiny messiahs of the bug world.

Water can boil and freeze at the same time (triple point). It's the drama queen of chemistry.

Mini Thought:

THat ugly ornament from 1984? It's family now. Deal with it.

While some traditions are passed down through generations, others start completely by accident – and stick around forever.

- Since 1997, one U.S. family has had every guest at their Christmas Eve dinner sign the same tablecloth as a keepsake.
- In Georgia (country), a traditional Christmas tree called the "chichilaki" is made from hazelnut or walnut branches – and kids believe it symbolises the tree of life.
- In Poland, some families still set an extra place at the table "for the unexpected guest" – a tradition rooted in hospitality and hope.
- In Sweden, the end of the Christmas season is marked on January 13 by "Knut's Party" (Julgransplundring) – people dance around the tree, strip off the decorations, and toss the tree out, literally "throwing out" Christmas.

Mini Thought:

no one remembers the expensive gifts. But everyone remembers who always burns the cinnamon rolls.

TRUE OR FALSE

? In Germany, children sometimes receive gifts from "The Christkind" instead of Santa Claus.

In India, it's common to decorate mango and banana trees for Christmas.

? In Portugal, some families set a place at the Christmas table for a deceased loved one.

In Argentina, Christmas is typically celebrated with hot cocoa and snowmen.

Bonus Fact Corner: Little But Legendary

In Denmark, many families leave out rice pudding for the Christmas gnome (nisse) – with a warning not to offend him.

In the U.S., the "ugly sweater family photo" has become a holiday staple – often more competitive than the actual gifts.

In Iceland, people gift books on Christmas Eve and spend the night reading – it's called Jólabókaflóð, or "Christmas Book Flood."

In Mexico, children take turns hitting a star-shaped piñata during Las Posadas – a joyful tradition full of singing and candy.

FUN FACT QUICKFIRE: *Final Festive Edition*

- Ukraine: It's common to decorate Christmas trees with spider webs – symbolizing good luck and inspired by local folklore.
- Ethiopia: Christmas (Genna) is celebrated on January 7th with a traditional fasting period beforehand and a game called genna, similar to field hockey.
- Colombia: Dia de las Velitas (Day of the Little Candles) kicks off the season on December 7 with thousands of candles lighting up streets and windows.
- Venezuela: In Caracas, it's tradition to roller-skate to early morning Christmas Mass – some streets are even closed to cars for it.
- Philippines: The Simbang Gabi tradition involves attending nine pre-dawn masses before Christmas, often followed by hot drinks and sweet rice cakes.

End-of-Day Wisdom

YOU DON'T NEED PERFECT HOLIDAYS. YOU NEED YOUR HOLIDAYS.
THE TINIEST TRADITIONS OFTEN LEAVE THE BIGGEST FOOTPRINTS IN OUR HEARTS.

The Christmas Aftermath

Main Trivia #1: The Gift Returns Boom

In the U.S., retailers expect about 17% of holiday purchases to be returned following the season – that translates into tens of billions of dollars worth of goods heading back. Key return-rush days typically span Dec 26 to Dec 28, when stores and online portals see their highest return volumes. The most commonly returned gifts? Clothing, shoes, and electronics, especially items bought in a last-minute panic. And yes – "wrong size," "wrong color," and "what were they thinking?" are all unofficial categories.

While many countries treat December 26 as a quiet holiday (like Boxing Day in the UK and Canada), Americans often hit the return queue early – armed with gift receipts, apologies, and determination.

💪 Christmas Table Flex:

One in ten people admits to re-gifting at least one present every year – sometimes before the wrapping paper cools.

TOTALLY USELESS RECORDS YOU DIDN'T ASK FOR

Snails have thousands of microscopic teeth.
Just don't ask them to chew faster.

Orange carrots are not original – the first were purple.
So carrots went through a branding phase.

Mini Thought:

It's not re-gifting.
It's eco-conscious emotional recycling.

The holidays are supposed to be joyful... but according to surveys, they're also a prime time for family drama. One UK poll found that nearly 1 in 5 people expect at least one major argument during Christmas celebrations. Common triggers include money, unhelpful in-laws, cooking disasters, and age-old feuds reignited by board games. In the U.S., therapists report a spike in calls right after the holidays, often linked to "festive tension." Add travel stress, alcohol, and overcooked turkey, and suddenly even "Silent Night" feels ironic.

Apparently, "peace on Earth" doesn't always apply to the dining room.

Mini Thought

"If you made it through Christmas without arguing about politics, in-laws, or who ruined the gravy - you're basically a festive Jedi."

Bonus Fact Corner: The Season of Sudden Regret

In the UK, around £1 billion worth of unwanted gifts are received every Christmas, with many resold or donated within days.

January is the busiest month for breakups on dating apps - often spurred by holiday stress or unmet expectations.

The U.S. sees a dramatic spike in store returns on December 26, nicknamed "National Return Day."

In Canada, one survey showed that nearly 40% of people feel "relieved" when Christmas is over - more than those who said they felt sad.

FUN FACT QUICKFIRE: *Post-Christmas Panic Edition*

- The first week of January is when gyms report the highest spike in new memberships – followed closely by the steepest drop in attendance.
- Google searches for "how to return a gift" peak on December 26, often alongside "can I return opened perfume?"
- "Festive burnout" is a real term used in psychology, describing the emotional crash after prolonged holiday pressure.
- In 2021, over 50% of shoppers admitted they'd kept at least one gift they hated just to avoid hurting someone's feelings.
- The top trending scent for post-Christmas candles? "Clean linen." Apparently, people are emotionally done with cinnamon.
- A study in the U.S. predicted that Americans would spend around $10.1 billion on unwanted gifts in 2024, with 53% of adults expecting to receive at least one disappointing present.

MINI QUIZ - SANTA OR SCAMMER?
Which one's true?

A. Searches for "how to rewrap gifts" peak on New Year's Eve.

B. Google searches for "how to return a gift" peak on December 26.

C. January 1 is statistically the day most people start journaling… and stop.

End-of-Day Wisdom

The gifts are unwrapped, the relatives have left, and your fridge is now 80% leftovers and regret.
Christmas isn't really over - it just goes into refund mode.
Take a breath, sip something warm, and remember: the best parts of the holidays are rarely the ones you planned.

Day 1 Quiz Answers:
1. The first artificial Christmas trees were made of goose feathers.
2. The world's tallest Christmas tree was in Finland.
3. "Jingle Bells" was originally written for Thanksgiving.
4. Candy canes were invented by a choirmaster to keep kids quiet during mass.
Answers:
1 – True (The earliest artificial trees appeared in 19th-century Germany and were crafted from dyed goose feathers attached to wire branches. They were an eco-friendly alternative to cutting down live trees.)
2 – False (The record-holding tallest Christmas tree was a 221-foot Douglas fir set up in Seattle, USA, in 1950 – not in Finland.)
3 – True ("Jingle Bells" was written by James Lord Pierpont in 1857 for a Thanksgiving service, only later becoming a Christmas classic.)
4 – True (In 17th-century Germany, a choirmaster gave bent sugar sticks to children during mass to keep them quiet – the start of the candy cane tradition.)

DAY 2 Mini Quiz Answers: Answers: A – 1. Japan B – 2. Sweden C – 3. Ukraine D – 4. Norway E – 5. Mexico

Day 6 Quiz Answers:
1. The first Christmas card was sent in 1843.
2. "Silent Night" was written in German, not Latin.
3. Rudolph was invented by Coca-Cola.
4. In Poland, people open gifts on Christmas Eve, not Christmas Day.
Answers:
1 – True (The first commercial Christmas card was designed and printed in London in 1843 by John Callcott Horsley for Sir Henry Cole, who wanted a festive way to encourage people to use the postal service.)
2 – True ("Silent Night" – or Stille Nacht – was originally written in German in 1818 by Joseph Mohr and Franz Xaver Gruber in Austria.)
3 – False (Rudolph the Red-Nosed Reindeer was created in 1939 by Robert L. May as part of a holiday promotion for Montgomery Ward, not Coca-Cola.)
4 – True (In Poland, it's traditional to open presents on Christmas Eve after the festive dinner known as Wigilia, not on December 25th.)

Day 6 Mini Quiz:
Answer: B – the Olympia SnowWoman in Maine, USA.

Day 7 Quiz Answers:
1. "Elf" was partly filmed in New York without permits.
2. Jim Carrey trained with a Navy SEAL to survive the Grinch costume.
3. The snow in "Home Alone" was made from potato flakes.
4. The cottage from "The Holiday" is a real house in England.

Answers:

1 – True (Scenes of Buddy walking through NYC were filmed guerrilla-style without permits. Real pedestrians and reactions were captured spontaneously.)

2 – True (Jim Carrey underwent training with a Navy SEAL to help him endure the intense, claustrophobic Grinch makeup process, which took over 8 hours to apply.)

3 – True (The snow used in Home Alone included biodegradable potato flakes for close-ups and scenes requiring crunch underfoot.)

4 – False (The adorable cottage from The Holiday was a movie set built just for the film – it's not a real house, though it was inspired by real English cottages.)

Day 8 Mini Quiz:
Answer: B – The 1843 Christmas card by Sir Henry Cole really did scandalize Victorians because it showed a child holding a glass of wine.

Day 9 Mini Quiz:
Answer: D – In 2019, in Germany, a 600-meter-long Christmas table hosted over 2,000 diners in a record-breaking community feast.

DAY 10 True or False – Global Christmas Creatures & Traditions
   1. Reindeer noses turn red in winter because of extra blood flow.
   2. The Yule Cat legend was invented in the 2000s as a joke.
   3. Norway sends a Christmas tree to London every ten years.
   4. A penguin once delivered gifts to kids in New Zealand.
Answers:

1 – True (Reindeer have a dense network of blood vessels in their noses to help regulate temperature, which can cause a reddish tint.)

2 – False (The Yule Cat, or Jólakötturinn, comes from 19th-century Icelandic folklore and is definitely older than the 2000s.)

3 – False (Norway sends a Christmas tree to London every year as a thank-you for WWII support.)

4 – True (In 2009, a costumed penguin in a New Zealand zoo helped deliver gifts to children during a festive event.)

DAY 12 TRUE OR FALSE – Christmas Close Calls Edition
- The White House once had a Christmas tree fire while the president was inside.
- A German police call turned out to be caused by a sleeping hedgehog.
- Rio's floating Christmas tree once caught fire during a storm.
- A man cooked his Christmas dinner with a space heater on purpose.

Answers:

1 — True (1929, Herbert Hoover's tree).

2 — True (2018, Bavaria).

3 — True (2013, lightning strike).

4 — False (it was a hair dryer accident in 2020).

Day 13 True or False — Holiday Hustle Edition

1. There's a professional "turkey taste tester" job in the UK.
2. The world's most expensive Santa suit cost over $10,000.
3. Finland trains its mall Santas at a national Santa academy.
4. The first paid Santa appearance was in a New York store in 1890.

Answers:

1 — True (Major UK poultry brands hire seasonal "turkey taste testers" for quality control before Christmas.)

2 — True (A custom Santa suit made with Swarovski crystals and Italian silk reportedly sold for over $10,000.)

3 — True (Finland's official Santa Claus School operates in Lapland, training Santas for tourism and mall work.)

4 — False (It was actually in Brockton, Massachusetts, in 1890 — James Edgar was the first professional Santa.)

DAY 14 True or False — Holiday Science Edition

1. The "smell of snow" comes from ozone released in cold air.
2. Christmas tree needles can conduct small amounts of electricity.
3. Eating gingerbread can improve your reaction time.
4. NASA once tracked Santa using a radar glitch.

Answers:

1 — True (Ozone and petrichor compounds become more noticeable in cold, dry air.)

2 — False (They contain moisture but don't conduct electricity in measurable amounts.)

3 — True (Spices like ginger and cinnamon can increase alertness and blood circulation.)

4 — True (NORAD's Santa Tracker started in 1955 after a radar misdial by a child — and NASA later joined in the fun.)

DAY 15 True or False — Christmas in Orbit Edition

- Apollo 8 astronauts brought a small Bible to space.
- The first Christmas tree in orbit was made of wires and Velcro.
- No Christmas music has ever been played in space.
- Santa has been officially tracked by NORAD since the 1950s.

Answers:

1 – True (They read from Genesis using a small Bible onboard.)

2 – True (Skylab 3 astronauts built one from food containers and foil in 1973.)

3 – False (Holiday songs have been played on every ISS Christmas.)

4 – True (The NORAD Santa Tracker began in 1955 and still operates annually.)

DAY 16 Answers:

1 – b) Christmas Eve   2 – a) Toilet seat   3 – a) December 26   4 – b) Germany

DAY 17 Answers:

1 – b) Christmas pudding   2 – b) Norway   3 – b) Bryan, Texas   4 – b) KFC

Day 18 Mini Quiz – Lost & Found Edition:

Answer: A – A postcard from 1919 was delivered in the UK over a century later.

Day 20 Mini Quiz – Santa or Scammer?

Answer: B – In Ireland, a Santa parachute stunt went wrong, and he crash-landed mid-golf tournament. Ho-ho-nope.

DAY 21 — TRUE OR FALSE

1. The first electric Christmas tree lights were powered by a car battery.
2. The NORAD Santa Tracker started because of a wrong phone number.
3. AI once wrote a Christmas song that accidentally sounded like a funeral hymn.
4. 3D printers have been used to make edible Christmas cookies.

Answers:

1 – True. Early electric tree lights were indeed powered using car batteries before home electricity was common.

2 – True. In 1955, a misprinted phone number in an ad led children to call NORAD, creating the Santa Tracker tradition.

3 – True. Experimental AI models have produced Christmas music that unintentionally sounded haunting and mournful.

4 – False. While 3D-printed food exists, it hasn't become a real method for making traditional Christmas cookies.

DAY 22 True or False – Animal Chaos Edition

1. Some towns in the U.S. host "Santa Paws" events where pets take photos with Santa.
2. A parrot once sang "Jingle Bells" live on radio and then cursed at the host.

3. In the Czech Republic, people organize nativity church services for their hamsters.
4. Cats are biologically drawn to Christmas trees due to the smell of pine sap.
Answers:
1 – True. Malls and shelters across the U.S. host "Santa Paws" events where pets get photos with Santa – and sometimes treats too.
2 – True. Parrots are great mimics. There are documented cases (including one in Canada) where a bird sang carols and cursed during radio or livestreams.
3 – False. There's no such thing as official hamster nativity services in the Czech Republic. Yet.
4 – False. Cats attack Christmas trees mostly out of curiosity and for climbing fun – not because of pine sap chemistry.

DAY 23 True or False – Christmas Across the Clock
1. In Samoa, Christmas happens before it does in most of Australia.
2. In Greece, Orthodox Christmas is celebrated only on January 7th.
3. You could spend Christmas morning in New Zealand and Christmas night in Hawaii – on the same date.
4. Bethlehem celebrates Christmas with a live camel parade through the streets.
Answers:
1 – True. Samoa is one of the first places on Earth to ring in Christmas, ahead of most countries – including most of Australia.
2 – False. While many Orthodox churches follow the Julian calendar (and celebrate on January 7th), the Greek Orthodox Church celebrates Christmas on December 25th.
3 – True (in theory). With a time difference of up to 23 hours, you could technically experience Christmas morning in New Zealand, hop on a fast flight, and still catch Christmas night in Hawaii.
4 – False. While festive processions happen in Bethlehem, camels aren't part of an official street parade.

DAY 24 True or False – Family Rituals Edition
1. In Germany, children sometimes receive gifts from "The Christkind" instead of Santa Claus.
2. In Portugal, some families set a place at the Christmas table for a deceased loved one.
3. In India, it's common to decorate mango and banana trees for Christmas.
4. In Argentina, Christmas is typically celebrated with hot cocoa and snowmen.

Answers:

1 – True. In many German-speaking areas, Christkind (a Christ child–like figure) brings gifts instead of Santa.

2 – True. In some regions of Portugal, families honor the dead by including them in the Christmas meal.

3 – True. Especially in southern India, families decorate local trees like mango or banana for the holidays.

4 – False. Christmas in Argentina falls in summer – people celebrate with fireworks, barbecues, and cold drinks.

DAY 25 MINI QUIZ: Which one's true?
Correct answer: B – Search data shows a sharp spike for "how to return a gift" right after Christmas – turns out regret logs in faster than the warranty.

Printed in Dunstable, United Kingdom

72225177R00047